The Washington Monument

by Kristin L. Nelson

Lerner Publications Company • Minneapolis

To everyone who believes in someone enough to never give up

Text copyright © 2003 by Kristin L. Nelson

This book is available in two editions:
Library binding by Lerner Publications Company, a division of Lerner Publications Group
Soft cover by First Avenue Editions, an imprint of Lerner Publishing Group
241 First Avenue North
Minneapolis, MN 55401 USA

Website address: www.lernerbooks.com

Words in **bold type** are explained in a glossary on page 31.

Library of Congress Cataloging-in-Publication Data

Nelson, Kristin L.
      The Washington Monument / by Kristin L. Nelson.
          p.   cm. – (Pull ahead books)
      Includes index.
      Summary: An introduction to the purpose, structure, and history of the Washington Monument.
      ISBN: 0–8225–0250–X (lib. bdg. : alk. paper)
      ISBN: 0–8225–3759–1 (pbk. : alk. paper)
      1. Washington Monument (Washington, D.C.)–Juvenile literature.
      2. Washington Monument (Washington, D.C.)–History–Juvenile literature. 3. Washington (D.C.)–Buildings, structures, etc.–Juvenile literature. [1. Washington Monument (Washington, D.C.) 2. National monuments.] I. Title. II. Series.
      F203.4.W3 N45 2003
      975.3–dc21   2002013949

Manufactured in the United States of America
1 2 3 4 5 6 – JR – 08 07 06 05 04 03

What is the tallest
stone building in
Washington, D.C.?

It is the Washington Monument.

The **monument** was built to honor George Washington. He is known as the father of our country.

In the 1770s, America was ruled by England. Americans had to fight a war for their freedom.

They chose George Washington to lead their army. He was a brave soldier and a strong leader.

The Americans won the war. The
United States became a new country.
George Washington was a hero.

He was elected the first **president** of the United States.

Americans wanted to name the **capital** city for George Washington. It was named Washington, D.C.

Years later, they wanted to build a
monument to honor Washington. It would
be a **symbol** of their leader's strength.

In 1845, Robert Mills was hired to plan
the monument. He planned a round
building around an **obelisk** tower.

The workers only
built the obelisk
tower. The
round building
was never made.

19

Inside, the workers built a stairway up to the top. They built an elevator, too.

People from around the world gave **memorial stones.** The stones were placed in the walls of the monument's stairway.

In 1884, the monument was finally
finished!

About one million people visit the
Washington Monument every year. They
come to honor George Washington.

At the bottom of the monument,
50 flags wave. They stand for the
50 states.

Have you ever been to the top of the monument? You can see all around Washington, D.C.

The Washington Monument stands tall and strong like our country's first president.

It is a symbol of George Washington,
the father of our country.

Facts about the Washington Monument

- The Washington Monument is 555 feet high. That is twice as tall as the United States Capitol building.

- The monument's elevator takes about one minute to go from bottom to top. It has glass doors so you can see the memorial stones in the stairway.

- If the winds are strong enough, the monument sways slightly.

- A year after the monument was completed, it was struck by lightning. Only one of the outside stones was destroyed. But some equipment inside the monument was damaged and had to be replaced.

- Between 1997 and 2001, workers cleaned the monument and made it look like new.

- The monument, the U.S. capital, 7 mountains, 10 lakes, and over 100 towns are named after George Washington.

Memorial Stones

Memorial stones were donated by 41 states, 19 American cities, 12 countries, and many organizations. You can see them in the stairway or from the elevator.

The Pope donated a memorial stone in 1854. Not long after, the stone was stolen. It has never been found.

More about
the Washington Monument

Books

Adler, David A. *A Picture Book of Washington, D.C.* New York: Holiday House, 1990.

D'Aulaire, Ingri, and Edgar Parin D'Aulaire. *George Washington.* Garden City, NY: Doubleday, 1936.

Munro, Roxie. *The Inside-Outside Book of Washington, D.C.* New York: Dutton, 1987.

Ransom, Candice. *George Washington.* Minneapolis: Lerner Publications, 2002.

Websites

Ben's Guide to U.S. Government for Kids—Symbols
<http://bensguide.gpo.gov/3-5/symbols/index.html>

Capital Cam—Washington, D.C.
<http://www.earthcam.com/usa/dc/metrosquare/>

Washington Monument—National Park Service
<http://www.nps.gov/wamo/home.htm>

Visiting the Washington Monument

The Washington Monument is at the west end of the National Mall in Washington, D.C. It is open to visitors year-round.

Glossary

capital: a city where a government is based. Washington, D.C., is the capital of the United States.

marble: a hard stone with colored patterns in it. It is used for buildings and sculptures.

memorial stones: stones engraved with words to remind people of a place or an organization or an event

monument: a building or statue that reminds people of an event or a person

obelisk: a 4-sided pillar that is topped by a pyramid

president: the leader of a country, such as the United States

symbol: an object that stands for an idea, a country, or a person

Index

Photo Acknowledgments

The pictures in this book have been reproduced with the permission of: Corbis Royalty Free Images, pp. 3, 17, 24; © Bachmann/Photo Network, p. 4; Library of Congress, pp. 5, 7, 9; © North Wind Picture Archives, pp. 6, 8, 10, 11, 13, 18, 20; *Dictionary of American Portraits,* p. 12; © Brown Brothers, pp. 14, 22, 27; National Archives, pp. 15, 16, 19; © Rick Latoff/Photri, pp. 21, 29 (both); © Richard T. Nowitz/CORBIS, p. 23; © CORBIS, p. 25; © Ferrell McCollough/SuperStock, p. 26.

Cover photo used with the permission of © A. A. M. Van der Heyden/Independent Picture Service.